The *Fragrant Flowers*
BIRTHDAY BOOK

Books by Jacqueline Hériteau and Susan Davis
The Fragrant Flowers Birthday Book
A Feast of Flowers

Books by Jacqueline Hériteau
Water Gardens, with Charles Thomas
The National Arboretum Book of Outstanding Garden Plants
The American Horticultural Society Flower Finder
A Feast of Soups
Potpourri and Other Fragrant Delights

The Fragrant Flowers BIRTHDAY BOOK

Jacqueline Hériteau
and
Susan Davis

A Judd Publishing Book

Houghton Mifflin Company
Boston New York
1994

A Judd Publishing Book.

Library of Congress Cataloging-in-Publication Data
Hériteau, Jacqueline
The fragrant flowers birthday book/Jacqueline Hériteau and Susan Davis

p.   cm.

ISBN 0-395-70564-9

Printed in Hong Kong

Book design by Barkin & Davis, Inc.

Contents

Introduction

FRAGRANT BIRTHDAY FLOWERS

Fragrant flowers make the most welcome birthday gifts. The rustle of silky florist's paper, that first glimpse of satin petals nestled in greens, light up the day. Unwrapping potted hyacinths or a gardenia plant in bloom, you are enfolded in the sweet scent of woodlands and wildflowers, mosses and streams, skies and bees and butterflies, gardens in the sun. When the flower you give shares the birthday of the person receiving it, the gift becomes magical.

A plant's birthday is its high season, when its flowers come out in its native climate. We've used the high season of the most beautiful perfume flowers in cultivation to create a fragrant birthday year. By dividing each month into four parts, this birthday book becomes a perpetual calendar.

At the time of the birthday, most of these gorgeous blossoms are available by the stem, in pots, or as seedlings from florists, garden centers, or mail order nurseries. Many can be brought into bloom in your own garden or greenhouse or on a sunny windowsill. A few of the exotics that are assigned to birthdays in the cold months may be harder to find, but they are too wonderful to leave out. Depending on your location, you may have to special-order cut flowers of a tropical such as frangipani. But you can also grow a tropical plant in a container that summers outdoors and winters in a frost-free garage or basement.

With each flower we have provided space for recording its birthday people, along with a description of the blossom. We've also included a potpourri of facts and fantasies associated with the flower. Pass these along to the birthday recipient to make the gift more meaningful.

When the world was new, people found real magic in the perfumed flowers. Potions of sweetbrier were taken to keep bodies healthy; lilies were made into salves that soothed pain. The fragrant flowers made life richer: apple blossoms lifted the spirit; carnations flavored food; sweet violets inspired poets. And some flowers made people rich. The tulips that were just ordinary flowers in the opulent winter gardens of Suleiman the Magnificent were imported and improved by the Dutch and sold for unimaginable sums.

In recent centuries, brave and besotted plant explorers have risked their lives again and again in far-off lands to bring us exquisite specimens like winter daphne, sweet olive, and other perfumed plants we've included to round out the fragrant year. The everblooming quality of modern roses is a gift of the species that plant explorers sent rocking across the South Seas on the grand old China clippers.

Magic spells are still cast by a truly fragrant flower, especially one that blooms for your birthday. It can speak to you: in the ancient language of the flowers a rose stands for love, a lily for purity, and hyacinths for eternal renewal. A flower's story can add romance to your life: the mythology of its native land, the people who loved it, the meaning it once held, weave lovely patterns in the fabric of your thought. Its perfume delights. Its beauty shines in your eyes.

Long after the last sweetly scented petal has fallen, a fragrant birthday flower lingers in your heart.

Happy Birthday!
Jacqueline Hériteau and Susan Davis
Washington, D.C.

Hyacinth

An ancient Persian proverb says, "If you have two coins, use one to buy bread and the other to buy hyacinths for the joy of your spirit."

For the first birthday of the year, give a potful of one of the most fragrant flowers on earth. A symbol of eternal renewal, when winter is at its dreariest, a pot of forced hyacinths wafts a sweet, rich, satiny perfume through the air. This cone of starry, outfacing bells in pastel colors is one of the ancient flowers. Hyacinths perfumed Homer's carpet of the gods and bloomed in the meadows of ancient Greece as Pan and the nymphs passed, singing. The flower is named for Hyacinthus, a Greek hero loved by Apollo, the sun. Slain by the jealous West Wind, Hyacinthus sank to the underworld, but when spring comes, Hyacinthus returns and love blossoms.

Though hyacinths won't flower in northern gardens until spring, they bloom in winter in their native lands, the valleys and foothills of the eastern Mediterranean. In the mid-1500s, the Austrian ambassador to Persia was entranced by the perfumed bulb flowers he found blooming in winter in the court of Suleiman the Magnificent. By the end of the century they had reached Holland, and a thriving national industry was established. The extraordinary fragrance of the hyacinth soon made it Europe's flower of high fashion.

In midwinter you'll find pots of dainty French and Roman varieties, *Hyacinthus orientalis* var. *albulus,* at florists and garden centers. These early varieties have been forced into bloom. Include a note with your gift suggesting that the bulb be planted in the garden in warmer weather. A forced hyacinth often comes back the following spring. The forced hyacinth blooms for only a

*To
have a supply of
hyacinths for gifts, in mid- to
late fall start bulbs in hyacinth
glasses. Among the best for forcing
are 'L'Innocence', 'Pink Pearl',
and 'King of Blues'.*

week or two, but you can extend the birthday gift by giving several more hyacinths. In a few weeks, pots of the big Dutch hyacinths will be available. Then bulbs planted in the garden the previous fall will bloom; when the buds color, pot them up and bring them indoors to bloom.

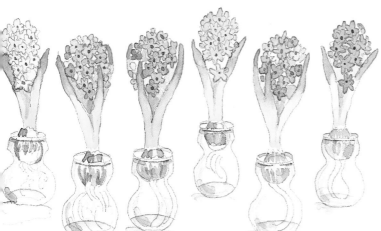

*Birthdays January 1-7
Day & Year*

_____

_____

_____

_____

_____

Carnation

This bright and cheerful flower is a treat for a wintry birthday, full of good omens and "greatly comforting those that are sick...of any disease where the heart need relief." Medieval artists thought of the fluffy, ruffled carnation as one of the "divine flowers" that grow in paradise. Patience, gentleness, gallantry, refinement, and comfort are qualities associated with it, perhaps because it stays fresh for the longest time even after being cut. As early as 300 B.C., the carnation was treasured for its rich, sharp, sweet scent of cloves and fine blue-green foliage. In the sixteenth and seventeenth centuries, its fragrance was considered second only to that of the rose.

The large florist's carnation *Dianthus caryophyllus* and its charming cousins the pinks are the edible "clove gilly-flowers" listed in the old keeping-room recipes. The Elizabethans used them as spice and medication, for they believed that a nibble or two of this birthday flower could lift the recipient's soul and spirit and keep bad dreams away. Carnations were served in wine — "sops in wine" — in mutton sauce, syrups, and candied and pickled. A kind of cologne known as gilliflower vinegar was "used in times of contagious diseases, and...for such as have feeble spirits."

Flower markets will offer you dozens of carnations in sparkling colors that will make a birthday bouquet. The long-stemmed miniatures

are so inexpensive, you can give an armful and still feel rich. Carnations are gorgeous against the dark green of ferns or the bold foliage of aucuba. Recut and placed in water containing floral preservative, carnations will remain beautiful for ten days to two weeks. Even the side buds will open.

For a child's birthday, give a seed packet of the easily grown and very fragrant little pinks to plant in the garden or in a window box in the spring. The Allwood pinks, 'Cinnamon Pink' and 'Lady Granville', and the Cheddar pink, *Dianthus gratianopolitanus,* are highly scented. Wrap the seeds and top the package with a bow and a fresh miniature carnation.

15

Orange Blossoms

This birthday flower crowns June brides, but right now is when the little citrus plants that bear them are starting to bloom in indoor gardens, in greenhouses, and in orchards in warm regions.

Gold-centered and pure white, the orange blossom is an age-old floral symbol for purity. The rich, fruity, sweet fragrance is the world's favorite scent, one of the extraordinary "signature" perfumes used to describe other scents. Track orange blossoms as they spread around the globe and you'll have a history of the world to give as a present. Before Christ walked the hills of Galilee, Persia traded grapes and horses to obtain orange trees — and their fragrant blossoms — from China. When the Moors conquered Spain in the seventh century, they planted orange trees in the Persian gardens they created at Córdoba: the Patio de los Naranjos (Court of the Oranges) still survives beside the cathedral. France's Sun King, Louis XIV, so loved the fragrance he had hundreds of orange trees planted in sterling silver pots and scattered around the palace of Versailles. The Spanish introduced oranges to Florida in 1579. In the eighteenth century neroli oil, the essential oil extracted from orange blossoms, was one of the most valued ingredients in perfume.

Florists use orange blossoms in bridal work even if they don't stock them, and they can order flowers for you. Make this gift different: have the florist create a bracelet or a nosegay of fresh orange blossoms.

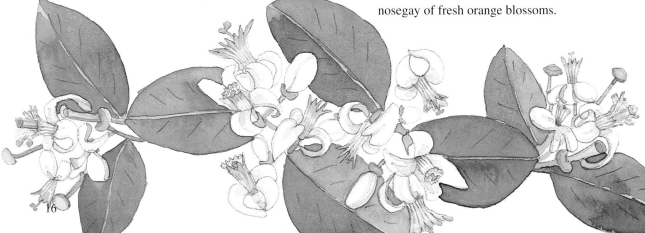

Potted citruses are beautiful, long-lived plants; there's a rumor that six of the original trees from Louis XIV's *orangerie* are still with us! And this is a gift you can grow yourself simply by planting seeds from citrus fruit.

Florists and garden markets sell fragrant citruses to grow indoors. Among the best for scent are these four:

The sweet orange, *Citrus sinensis,* has been the floral symbol of Florida since 1907; it bears fragrant flowers and sweet fruits.

The small calamondin or Panama orange, *X Citrofortunella mitis,* produces masses of tiny fragrant blossoms followed by small, round orange-yellow fruits that make excellent marmalade.

Otaheite or Tahiti orange, *Citrus taitensis,* a little shrub, bears fragrant flowers and two-inch fruits.

Citrus limoni 'Ponderosa' produces large and wonderfully fragrant flowers from mid-January until summer, followed by large fruits. Even the twigs and leaves of this plant are used in perfumery.

*Birthdays January 16-23
Day & Year*

_____

_____

_____

_____

17

Camellia

The most beautiful camellias are shaped like huge roses, but the waxy petals have a sculptural quality, a magical beauty, lasting freshness, and an imperial stillness that evokes reverence. When you give a red camellia, in the language of the flowers it says, "You are lovely." A white camellia stands for modesty and unassuming excellence. The scented species have a light bouquet, something like a sweet, exotic, delicate tea.

This birthday blossom is borne by a lovely little evergreen tree that flowers in winter — indoors in cool regions, outdoors where winters are mild. The camellia was the first flowering plant grown indoors in America, perhaps because it blooms so beautifully in cool rooms. The first species to reach the West came from Japan. In the late 1600s the flower captured artists and poets, heart and soul. Two centuries later it was immortalized by the French novelist and playwright Alexandre Dumas, *fils,* in the story of Camille, *La Dame aux Camélias* (*The Lady of the Camellias*).

Just one fabulous florist's camellia makes a breathtaking birthday gift. Be sure to ask for a fragrant variety, such as the red 'Bob Hope'.

A potted camellia is an even grander present. Two beautifully scented small-flowered species, *Camellia lutchuensis* and *Camellia sasanqua,* will grow indoors and are great in a greenhouse. On your gift card, suggest that the plant be kept close to a window. At the budding stage, camellias need cool air.

Camellia lutchuensis 'Fragrant Pink' bears masses of tiny, sweet-scented flowers like apple blossoms. The perfume of the cultivar called 'Scentuous' is likened to that of hyacinths.

A sasanqua camellia is more tolerant of warm rooms. Its flowers are dainty, lightly perfumed, and white or a lustrous shell pink.

Birthdays January 24-31
Day & Year

_____

_____

_____

_____

_____

Sweet Olive

This birthday week celebrates the sweet olive. It's an ideal signature flower for the person who appreciates the quiet power of enduring love — what the sweet olive represents.

The plant, *Osmanthus fragrans,* is a slow-growing shrub whose plain leaves look like a cross between holly and bay. The blossoms are small clusters of minuscule white florets that are almost invisible in the axils of the leaves. But the fragrance of these little blossoms is incomparable — sweet, fruity, like ripe nectarines or apricots, perhaps — and all out of proportion to the size of the florets. Just one or two will fill a house with fragrance. In China the florets are often used to perfume tea, which may account for one of its common names, tea olive.

The first sweet olive plant in the West was shipped from Canton, China, to Kew Gardens in England in 1770. It has been loved and cultivated so widely for so long that botanists are not sure of its exact point of origin.

In greenhouses and indoor gardens the sweet olive blooms from January or February until May or June. It repeats intermittently in the fall. Other species of osmanthus with more ornamental foliage are used in landscaping gardens where winters are mild. Some bloom most fully in early spring, others in fall.

A sprig of sweet olive in bloom with a large pink rose and a bit of white pine makes a sweetly fragrant little birthday bouquet. Or just tie the stem of the sweet olive with a white satin bow.

A sweet olive plant makes a wonderful gift, not only for its fragrance, but also because it is so attractive and undemanding. Include a note explaining that stuffy rooms bother it when the flower buds start to swell; it then needs cool air and high humidity.

Birthdays February 1-7
Day & Year

——————————————

——————————————

——————————————

——————————————

——————————————

21

FEBRUARY

Freesia

Refinement and subtlety characterize the freesia, and grace and a rich perfume make it especially appropriate for a Valentine's Day birthday gift. With its eight trumpets poised upward on the curved tip of a slim stem, this is one of the daintiest cut flowers we have. The trumpets open one or two at a time and fill a room with fragrance. When you give freesias, you are offering one of the finest known fragrances. Delicate, spicy, haunting, sweet, heady, lilylike — the adjectives used to describe the perfume are almost infinite, and inadequate.

The flowers develop from a cold-tender bulb that blooms from December to March in gardens in its native South Africa. It is a relative of the iris and fairly new to the West. Modern freesias are known as *Freesia X hybrida.* The original imports were *Freesia refracta* var. *alba.* The earliest freesias to bloom are generally creamy whites and pinks; the double-flowered hybrids are almost as fragrant. If you have a choice, pick yellow and orange freesias, which have a rich, fruity perfume. The violet and red varieties are generally less scented.

You'll have no trouble finding cut flowers, for florists stock freesias much of the year. For a birthday bouquet, select stems with just the first flower open and back them with a few dainty ferns. Ask the florist to tie them together with long, narrow satin ribbons that match the flower color.

If you find potted freesias just coming into bloom, choose them over the bouquet. Very few cut flowers can match the fragrance of flowers still attached to the plant. With notable exceptions (such as jasmine and tuberose), once flowers have been cut, they stop producing their essential perfume oils.

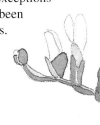

Birthdays February 8-14
Day & Year

_____

_____

_____

_____

_____

Daffodil

Receiving a big bunch of daffodils is like having your arms filled with sunshine — a gorgeous gift for a February birthday. Greek legend says that Earth at the command of Zeus, god of the skies, brought forth the daffodil and "all wide heaven was filled with delight at the fragrance." Almost any large daffodil keeps a sweet, musky scent deep in its cup, but the truly fragrant one is the great yellow daffodil, a symbol of chivalry. The Greeks dedicated the flower to Persephone, queen of the underworld and goddess of agriculture, because the daffodil goes underground for a season and returns clothed in radiance.

The various *Narcissus* species first bloomed in the meadows in southeastern Europe and South Africa, but it was the Dutch who developed the modern plants that spread to the far corners of the world. By the early 1900s, most students could recite William Wordsworth's description of wandering in the Scottish Highlands "lonely as a cloud," chancing upon "a host of golden daffodils...fluttering and dancing in the breeze." At the end, the poet's heart is locked in eternal "dances with daffodils."

Though most of the early garden daffodils aren't ready to bloom yet, you'll find bunches of yellow gold for a birthday bouquet at flower markets.

Pots of forced daffodils are sold now; these are simply beautiful and will last longer than the cut flowers. On your card, include a note saying that these bulbs, like Persephone, will come back if they are planted in the garden after the foliage has ripened. They'll

Before combining freshly cut daffodils with other flowers, soak the stems in tepid water overnight. The toxic substance they exude is harmful to many other flowers.

likely bloom the next spring or the one after.
Or force the daffodils yourself. It's easy.
Pot chilled daffodil bulbs in the fall, and they'll bloom indoors in February. Choose fragrant cultivars like the large-flowered Trumpet (an all-time favorite) or 'King Alfred', which has the true fragrance of the yellow daffodil. The romantic Poetaz daffodil, 'Cragford', and double-flowered 'Cheerfulness' have heady scents. Golden 'Soleil d'Or' has a fruity perfume. Most Poeticus, or Pheasant's Eye, daffodils are deliciously spicy.

Birthdays February 15-21
Day & Year

_____

_____

_____

_____

Mimosa

Troubadours sang the praises of this birthday flower in the twelfth century, and modern poets have written odes to the tiny, sweetly scented but fleeting puffs of golden stamens. Honeyed mimosa, as elusive as the fragrance of the garden in sunlight, teases the senses with its undertone of sultry musk and wild grape. In the romantic literature of France, Germany, and Scandinavia, it is a symbol of love in spring and of secret love.

Mimosa is the blossom of the silver wattle tree, *Acacia decurrens* var. *dealbata,* a native of tropical Australia and the warm West Indies. In February in private gardens and nursery orchards in Provence, southern Florida, and California, the trees cover themselves with great cascades of the half-inch lemon pompoms. Commercial growers harvest the buds as they break and bring them into bloom in moist forcing chambers. Wrapped in silky tissue, they are flown to flower markets everywhere.

From February on, as long as the harvest lasts, you'll find sprays of mimosa backed by feathery blue-green foliage at florists. Mimosa with its foliage is especially lovely combined with a few yellow miniature roses. Have your gift enclosed in florist's paper before it leaves the shop. High temperatures, low humidity, and drafts quickly spoil the fluff of the cut flowers.

To keep mimosa beautiful, soak the stems for an hour or two in water acidified by a few drops of white vinegar or lemon juice. Then transfer the flowers to fresh tepid water containing floral preservative.

A potted mimosa will bloom indoors and grow into a beautiful six- or seven-foot tree. That's a gorgeous gift for the greenhouse or indoor gardener. Three species that bloom indoors and are available at flower shops or by mail are golden mimosa, *Acacia baileyana;* willowleaf acacia, *Acacia retinoides;* and silver-leaved mimosa, *Acacia dealbata.*

*Birthdays February 22-29
Day & Year*

_____

_____

_____

_____

_____

Scented Geranium

A scented geranium is like a big bouquet of delicately cut leaves that, at the slightest touch, release volumes of aromatic scent. The lacy little white, rose, or lilac flowers that appear in summer are also perfumed, though they are less strong.

There are hundreds of varieties, each claiming a different aroma. Some plants in the large rose-scented group smell so much like roses that they are used in perfumery. The citrus-scented group has delicious variations on the themes of lemon, lemon verbena, lemon drop candy, citronella, orange, and lime. Mint-scented geraniums abound. Others are identified with fruits and spices such as nutmeg, apricot, ginger, and strawberry, to name just a few.

They all belong to the *Pelargonium* genus, a group of tender perennials relatively new to the West. In the late 1600s, the rose-scented *Pelargonium capitatum* arrived. The pleasure and practical value of this plant and of the dozens of species that followed landed them on sunny windowsills and in greenhouses everywhere. Cuttings — which root easily — traveled west with the pioneers. Our great-grandmothers put them to all sorts of uses. The fresh leaves and flowers of rose-scented varieties flavored cakes, jellies, puddings, and sugar. Fresh citrus-scented varieties freshened finger and wash-bowls and polished furniture and wooden utensils. Dried rose- and lemon-scented leaves were used in potpourris and as room fresheners.

A birthday potful of young scented geraniums has an aroma as rich as a whole garden of fresh herbs. Combine three- to five-inch plants of several varieties. Include a card recommending winters in a sunny window and summers outdoors.

A lovely basic collection is 'Attar of Roses'; lemon-scented *Pelargonium crispum* var. *minor;* the peppermint or woolly *Pelargonium tomentosum,* which has large, soft, fuzzy leaves; and the velvety apple geranium, *Pelargonium odoratissimum.*

Old English Rose Bowl
7 cups fragrant rose petals, dried, 1 cup dried rosebuds, 1/2 cup dried rose geranium leaves, 1 ounce sandalwood raspings, 2 cups orris-root powder, 1/8 ounce oil of roses, 1/2 ounce oil of bergamot, 1/2 ounce oil of musk, 1/8 ounce oil of sandalwood.
Mix the dried roses, geranium leaves, and sandalwood raspings with the orris-root powder. As you mix, add the perfume oils a few drops at a time. Seal the container and allow the potpourri to cure in a dry, dark, warm room for six weeks. Stir the container daily to blend the oils.

Birthdays March 1-7
Day & Year

_____

_____

_____

_____

_____

29

Pittosporum

This birthday flower blooms on a beautiful evergreen shrub whose native lands are China and Japan. An emblem of devotion, loyalty, and lasting love, the little creamy white flower has a fragrance as heavenly as, and rather like, that of orange blossoms. The scent combines something sweet and lemony with an essence of Easter lilies, and the flowers remain for many, many weeks.

Where winters are cold, Japanese pittosporum, *Pittosporum tobira,* is an enormously successful houseplant that blooms at this season. It is often called "house mock orange," a reference to the similarity between its fragrance and that of *Philadelphus.*

Mock orange is the common name for *Philadelphus,* a big shrub whose beautiful white flowers and delicious fragrance are an unforgettable part of northern springtimes.

In warm regions, pittosporum's lustrous leaves and enduring beauty have made it a popular hedge plant. Depending on its location, it flowers between now and May. Australian laurel is a common name that refers to its handsome evergreen foliage.

You should be able to obtain branches or sprigs of Japanese pittosporum in bloom from a good flower shop in time for this birthday — or you may find it blooming in your own or a friend's garden. Pittosporum and masses of big white tulips make a fabulous birthday bouquet.

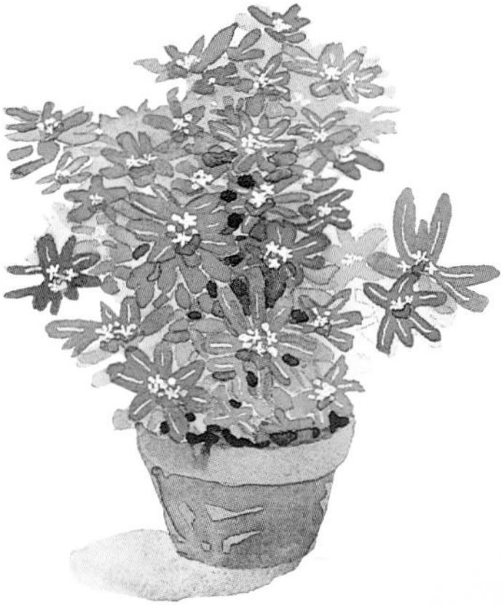

Birthdays March 8-15
Day & Year

A potted pittosporum is a great gift for the indoor gardener, especially a novice. It tolerates hot, dry locations, isn't particular about light, and can stand a wide range of temperatures. On your card, suggest a summer vacation for the plant in partial sun on a patio or balcony.

A variegated pittosporum with yellow margins is a beautiful foliage plant. It doesn't bloom as generously as the green form and so brings less perfume to the birthday party.

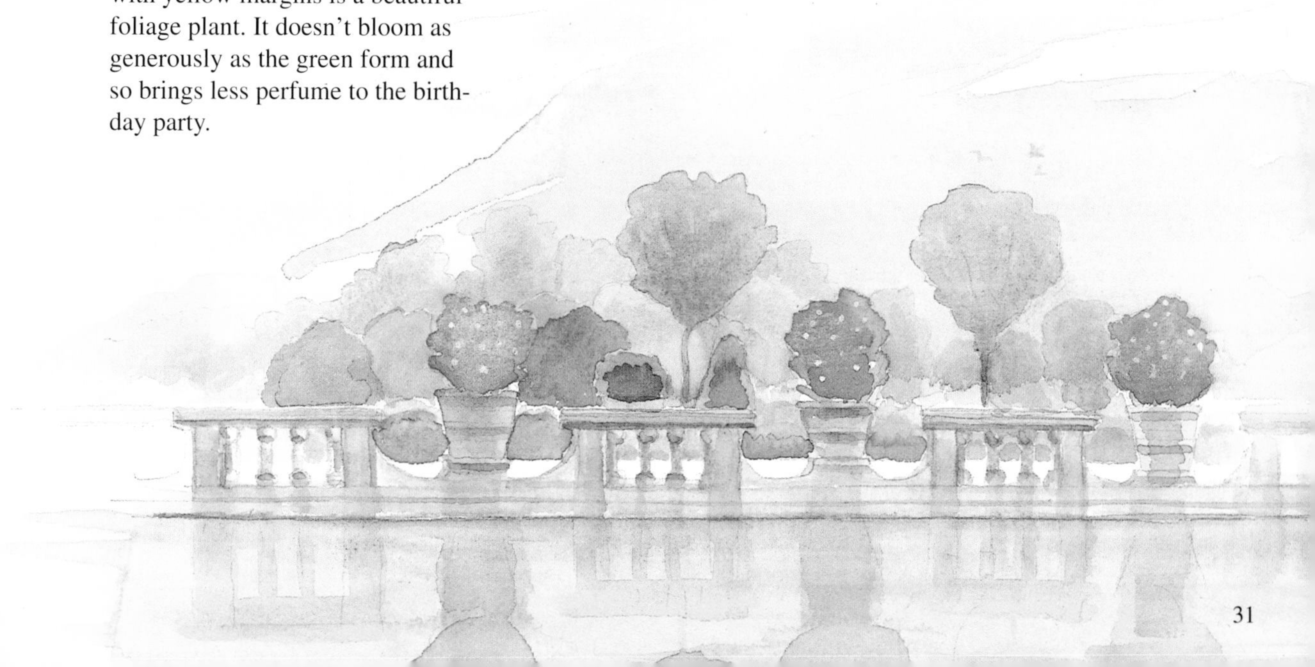

Easter Lily

Hauntingly perfumed, sweet as the sun on violets, a birthday gift of Easter lilies brings the scent of summer to the last days of winter. Flawless beauty belongs to this stately, pure white flower of light, which is forced into early bloom for the resurrection season. In the garden, it blooms in summer with the other lilies. An emblem of purity in religion and classical art, white lilies are the sign of the Virgin Mary. The angel Gabriel and Saint Catherine are often depicted holding lilies, symbols of the lives believers place in their care. Charlemagne honored the flower by naming it in his list of eighty-nine plants recommended for the municipalities he ruled.

For at least five thousand years the white Madonna lily, *Lilium candidum,* has been cultivated for its perfume. The fragrance is one of the great "signature" scents by which other floral fragrances are judged. Its beauty and medicinal uses came west with the Phoenicians and the Roman legions. Soldiers treated corns and the pain and inflammation of burns and scalds with ointments made from lily bulbs. To whiten skin, women applied solutions of water boiled with lily roots.

To make this birthday memorable for beauty, give a bouquet of lilies, blue delphiniums, and silvery pussy willows.

To make it memorable for fragrance, give a potted Easter lily. The species often forced for Easter is the gorgeous, highly perfumed *Lilium longiflorum* var. *eximium,* whose pure white is set off by a shower of golden stamens.

Birthdays March 16-23
Day & Year

_____

_____

_____

_____

_____

_____

On your card, include a note suggesting that the rootball be planted in the garden when the blooms have gone by. In warm regions, it may bloom again the very first summer. Suggest cutting the plant back to just above its foliage and planting it in full sun.

"Consider the lilies of the field, how they grow...And yet I say unto you, that even Solomon in all his glory was not arrayed like one of these."
Matthew 6:28-29

Fragrant Viburnum

Without this fragrant birthday blossom, spring to many gardeners would be like a bird without a song. The plant is a rather large, immensely popular landscape ornamental discovered early in this century in North China, where it was among the most treasured specimens of the imperial gardens in Pekin. Only after the fall of the dynasty did the plant come into the possession of everyday gardeners.

Fragrant viburnum brings to the last cold days of the year the season's most intoxicating perfume. The fragrance is released by rather sweet clusters of domed or rounded waxlike white or pinkish flowers. It recalls the sweetness of apple blossoms at noon and of honeysuckle, to which it is related. In summer fruits (drupes) form, and in fall the foliage of the best varieties turns coral and wine red.

Florists include branches of viburnum in lavish spring flower arrangements, but they don't stock it because it's so common in gardens. A pretty gift for this week's birthday is a small low arrangement of sprigs of viburnum and pink heather, with one very large pink tulip for color and some small-leaved ivy.

For a gardener, a viburnum plant is a gift filled with delightful promise. If the plant will end up in a greenhouse, choose the March-blooming, highly perfumed *Viburnum carlesii* or newer hybrids of this species.

If the viburnum will be planted in a garden, make your gift the most marvelously scented species, early-blooming *Viburnum farreri* (*Viburnum fragrans*). This species was

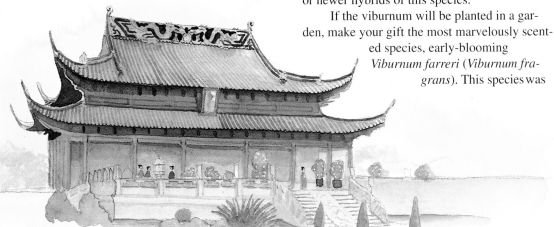

jealously guarded by the Chinese dowager empress. It develops buds between November and March and blooms for weeks or months. In areas where late frosts are a problem, a larger, somewhat less fragrant shrub, Judd viburnum, *Viburnum juddii,* is a safer choice.

Sweet Violet

The sweet violet is the perfumed species *Viola odorata,* a symbol of tender sentiments and virtuous modesty. The fragrance of this charming little birthday flower is unrivaled for sweetness, another of the "signature" scents that set standards for other florals. A source of perfume since ancient times, the sweet violet was the emblem of the Athens of antiquity and later scented dining room terraces in Rome. Both the Romans and Persians served wines flavored with sweet violets, and the Tudors of Britain went dotty over it. They perfumed honey with violets, administered violet paste and violet tea to the feeble,

and made violet syrups, conserves, and candies. We still do — and they make charming little birthday presents.

Romance has always been associated with this flower. A fragrant golden violet was the prize for the best love poem when troubadours were the heroes of the eleventh and twelfth centuries. Josephine de Beauharnais, the fascinating Creole who became Napoleon's empress, adored the violet-colored varieties. When she died, four years after their marriage was annulled, Napoleon had her grave planted over with her beloved flower. Before his final exile, he gathered violets from the grave and placed them in a locket, which he wore until his own

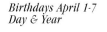

death a few years later, in 1821.

A nosegay of sweet violets surrounded by their leaves is a delightful, old-fashioned birthday gift. The plants are coming into bloom now in gardens where winters are mild, and some flower shops will have nosegays.

Or give a sweet violet plant. Nurseries specializing in fragrance carry some of the old favorites. 'White Czar', with large white flowers, and 'Royal Robe', with dark violet-blue, are among the best. 'Royal Robe' sometimes succeeds as a houseplant. The double Parma violet is considered to be the most desirable of all.

Just a packet of sweet violet seeds makes a charming gift. Planted now, they'll bloom next fall. Sweet violets may be easier to find in a catalogue than in a garden center.

The sense of smell is the most powerful of the senses, for it reaches and teaches the heart

Wallflower

This birthday week celebrates the wallflower, *Cheiranthus cheiri*. Sweetly perfumed and jewel-toned, its velvet blossoms brave the last of the cold to bloom in sun-warmed corners just about now. A symbol of fidelity in adversity, wallflowers glow in yellow, pink, orange, crimson, maroon, and white. Their perfume is astonishing — as sweet as roses and violets, as sensuous as lilies, and as spicy as cloves. The strength of the clove accent gave wallflowers the name wall-gilleflower (*girofle* is French for clove, *giroflée* for wallflower and stock). Double-flowered forms are the most fragrant.

A wildflower of southern Europe, *Cheiranthus* came to Western gardens so long ago the original species is lost. A fourteenth-century painting of a garden in paradise places wallflowers among the most important flowers of the time, roses and lilies. In his essay "Of Gardens," Francis Bacon recommends planting wallflowers under "a parlour or a lower chamber window" so that the pure sweet perfume will be wafted indoors. But it is more likely that they were grown with the medicinal herbs. An oil distilled from wallflowers and mixed with honey was recommended to treat ulcers, and drops of the juice were applied to improve dimming sight.

Bouquets of wallflowers turn up in some flower shops, and from late winter on seedlings in bloom are sold at garden markets. If you can't find the cut flowers, buy a plant and harvest your own to make a birthday nosegay. One or two stems of wallflower combined with small pink tulips and heather and tied with a matching ribbon make a delightful posy. It's a gift very much in line with the history of the flower: *Cheiranthus* means "handflower" — a name derived from the custom of adding wallflowers to perfume nosegays, which are held in the hand.

Wallflower seedlings aren't as pretty as a nosegay, but will last a lot longer. Planted now, they'll bloom until the weather gets hot, and they may return next year. In the moist northwestern United States, England, and much of Europe, wallflowers often perennialize.

In the Monet gardens at Giverny, yellow and red wallflowers are planted with lavender irises and tulips — a rich combination.

Birthdays April 8-15
Day & Year

_____

_____

_____

_____

_____

Apple Blossoms

Cup-shaped and delicate, arranged in charming clusters on their branches, apple blossoms make the most romantic birthday gift! The buds open from creamy white to blush pink, releasing a fragrance soft as mist, sweet as violets, light as almond, fruity as wild roses — spring's most adorable flowers. The blossoms have a pure, quiet beauty that stills the senses.

This flower belongs to legend. According to Celtic myth, King Arthur's magical Avalon was known as the "isle of apples." Elizabethans believed their "sweet perfumes work immediately upon the spirits...cheering and refreshing the Heart." Recent research on the positive effect of floral scents on health suggests that apple blossoms may have been ahead of their time.

Now and for the next several weeks, you will be able to buy branches of forced apple blossoms at flower markets. Their beauty is breathtaking, but the blossoms only hint at the fragrance of an apple tree in full bloom. Warmed by the sun, the flowers' early-morning hint of perfume intensifies and soon spreads far and wide. High noon buzzes with pollen-drunk bees. The scent dissipates in the cooling dusk until it is just a sweetness on the edge of consciousness. Probably the best birthday present you could give would be a picnic in an apple orchard.

An apple tree is a present that will last for decades. Choose one for its scent. Standard apple trees have a sweet fragrance, but some scented crabapples are divine. They are also small enough to thrive in containers on a balcony or patio.

The perfume of the Siberian flowering crabapple, *Malus baccata*, rivals that of the sweet violet, and birds love the bright fruits that follow.

The fragrant 'Dolgo' tolerates shade and cold winters. The scented blossoms of the beautiful little Japanese flowering crab, *Malus floribunda,* are spectacular — from deep pink to red in bud, pink fading to white as they open. The picturesque, scented tea crab, *Malus hupehensis,* has long, wandlike branches and is disease-resistant.

Birthdays April 16-23
Day & Year

_____
_____
_____
_____
_____

Once the buds swell, apple blossoms may be forced into early bloom. Cut and wrap the stems in damp newspaper and cure them in deep, cool water overnight before placing them in vases. They last longest in a cool room.

41

Peony

The voluptuous, openhearted peony is the most ancient of all cultivated flowers and the most opulent cut flower sold at this season. An armful of their white, cream, pink, or crimson gorgeousness makes a birthday gift of unsurpassed luxury. Most peonies have a sharp but slightly sweet, fresh aroma unlike any other. The scent of three or four peonies will make their presence known even in a large room. A few unusual varieties have the sweetness of a damask rose.

Paeonia, the botanical name for this fluffball of *peau-de-soie* petals, is derived from "paeon," as in "paeon of praise." To the Chinese of antiquity the peony was *sho yo*, "most beautiful," Queen of Flowers. The fourth month of the year was called "the moon of the peony." Both the Chinese and the Romans believed that peonies could heal various diseases and relieve depression. The Elizabethans went a step further and carried peony seeds as a charm against evil. On grand Victorian estates, the peony and the rose shared the role of supreme flower.

A peony wilted from lack of water may come back if it is recut and held under lukewarm water for a few minutes.

The peony, the longest-lived perennial plant we have, is a symbol for long life. There are peonies in China reputed to be two hundred years old.

A huge bouquet of peonies is a marvelous gift, but in the right setting even one of these breathtaking blossoms has immense appeal. For instance, float one magnificent peony in a crystal saucer, or nestle it in green moss in a corsage box. Peonies retain their freshness for more than a week if they are picked as the buds break. In water that is refreshed often, even tight buds open fully.

If the birthday belongs to a gardener, give a peony plant, which will bring you thanks year after year. Fluffy double peonies are the most fragrant. Known for their perfume are the rose-scented 'Vivid Rose', a late bloomer, and 'Festiva Supreme', a fluffy white whose central petals are tipped with red. Newly planted peonies go into full production in two or three years. In the hot South, plant early-flowering double peonies.

Birthdays April 24-30
Day & Year

_____

_____

_____

_____

_____

43

Lily-of-the-valley

 This intoxicatingly perfumed birthday flower is the beloved May lily, wood lily, or "fairy lamps of snow" of old folk tales. Its incomparable fragrance blends a fresh, light essence of lilies with the sweetness of violets in one of the world's greatest floral perfumes.

According to English legend, the lovely little white bells sprang up in the forest where Saint Leonard destroyed the dragons that were devastating Sussex. Where the flowers grow wild, this time of year woodsy slopes and sunny clearings are studded with their pointed tips. They unfurl a pair of broad grassy leaves from which a dainty stem rises bearing ten to twenty tiny bells. The fabulous perfume hovers over the fairy forest for most of the month.

Lily-of-the-valley, *Convallaria majalis,* grows wild throughout Eurasia, and has naturalized in North America. *Majalis* means "of May," and in France on May 1 lovers, friends, and co-workers celebrate by exchanging nosegays of lily-of-the-valley, which is an ancient symbol of the return of happiness. The first British record of lily-of-the-valley as a garden flower appeared in 1568. Its pure, fragrant little flowers were soon being prescribed to strengthen memory, to ease apoplexy, the pain of gout, and all sorts of ills. The flowers were also distilled in wine and brewed into lily-of-the-valley spirits.

At flower shops and garden markets this week you will find nosegays of lily-of-the-valley encircled by their

leaves. The ineffable perfume of one little bouquet will permeate a room and make the birthday memorable.

In winter and early spring, mail order catalogues offer forced lily-of-the-valley. They're adorable but provide only a whiff of the immaculate fragrance that scents the very expensive perfume called Joy.

If you can't find the real thing, give the perfume instead, lily-of-the-valley toiletries, or a sachet.

Birthdays May 1-7
Day & Year

_____

_____

_____

_____

_____

_____

Old Fashioned Lilac

Since colonial times this big shrub has been loved for its flowers and for its sweet, rich, distinctive fragrance, which saturates cool May evenings. All sorts of romantic and sentimental connotations are associated with this birthday flower. In the language of the flowers, purple lilac stands for the first emotions of love, white lilac for youthful innocence, wild lilac for humility. Lilacs in bloom mark the sites of farmhouses long gone and hedge the yards of historic New England villages. In the northern tier of America, lilacs are celebrated in spring festivals, and they have been immortalized in Walt Whitman's elegy to Lincoln, "When lilacs last in the dooryard bloom'd."

Originally from Asia and southeastern Europe, these fragrant flowers reached western Europe through Persia in the sixteenth century. John Gerard's *Herball* (1597), a catalogue of known plants, includes lilac as the "blue pipe privet." The popular small-flowered double varieties known as French lilacs were developed around 1875 by the French plantsman Victor

Lemoine. Their fragrance can be very sweet but can't compare with that of the old-fashioned common lilac, *Syringa vulgaris.*

You'll find all the lilacs you need for a fabulous birthday bouquet at flower markets right now. If you handle them the way florists do, they'll stay fresh for several days. First, remove all the foliage but the cluster of leaves nearest the flower. Then, with clippers or a sharp knife, recut the stems.

(Don't follow the old advice to mash them with a hammer!) Immediately place the stems in tepid water containing floral preservative.

For a gardener, a lilac bush is a present that will give a lifetime of pleasure. Look for a highly scented cultivar such as 'Mme. Lemoine', white; 'Edith Cavell', ivory-tinted; 'Belle de Nancy and 'Lavender Lady', lavender; 'Mrs. W. E. Marshall', pure purple; 'Mme. Antoine Buchner', double pink that fades to cool pink.

Birthdays May 8-15
Day & Year

Sweet Pea

The most adorable and refined of May's floral fragrances belongs to a pretty little thing that blooms on a pea vine, the annual sweet pea, *Lathyrus odoratus.* An old-fashioned flower, its scent is as soft as honeysuckle, as lovely as apple blossoms. The blooms top arched stems: puffs of petals like new silk in pastel salmon, pale yellow, blue, lavender, creamy white, darkest purple, navy, and ruby red.

A relative newcomer to our gardens, the sweet pea was introduced in the 1700s. Its fresh charm and delicate fragrance made it widely popular. A bouquet of sweet peas in mixed colors had no rival in the affections of the Victorian sweetheart. For those who spoke the language of the flowers, the sweet pea was a symbol of delicate pleasures, and of departure.

You'll find bouquets of sweet peas in delightful color mixes at florists and flower markets. Add a stem of asparagus fern, and bind the bouquet with long, narrow satin ribbons that match the sweet peas. Include a packet of floral preservative with your gift and suggest that the water be changed daily.

For a new gardener, a packet of sweet pea seeds is a welcome gift. It's too late to sow them this season, but the seeds will still be viable next March — and they're so easy to grow!

Birthdays May 16-23
Day & Year

_____

_____

_____

_____

_____

Fragrant Iris

The iris rewards close admirers with a whiff of honeyed fruit and something more — mimosa, perhaps. There are perfumed irises in every category, but the most memorable scents are wafted on May breezes by tall bearded irises such as the blue 'Scented Nutmeg', 'Victory Falls', and 'Blue Denim'; 'Baby Blessed', a light yellow dwarf bearded, has a sweet lemony perfume.

Irises are strong, sedate, and beautiful flowers that have long been symbols of hap-

piness, eloquence, serenity, and good news. They appeared on the walls of the Pyramids, served as food for Trojan orators who wished to achieve eloquence, and were pursued by Greeks seeking serenity. In classical Rome, Iris was the bearer of happy tidings, so as a reward Juno transformed her into the multicolored rainbow that announces the return of the sun. In the aromatic herb gardens of the Middle Ages, the iris was among the chief flowers — roses, lilies, carnations, wallflowers, and violets. The presence of an iris in Christian religious paintings was a sign of royal birth. The common name for the iris of Shakespeare's gar-

den, *Iris germanica,* is fleur-de-lis, the heraldic symbol of the French royal family.

At this time of year, irises are part of every bouquet. To make your birthday bouquet special, combine scented irises with flowers that are the very essence of spring — daffodils, narcissus, pink tulips, and pussy willows.

When choosing the irises, take those whose stems and bud tips are fresh and moist. Include a note with your gift explaining that the irises will last longer if the loose lower foliage is removed and they are placed in warm water containing floral preservative.

Orris root powder, which is used as a fixative for potpourris, pomanders, and dry perfumes, is the ground root of dried Iris germanica *var.* florentina, *the scented two-toned purple flag.*

Birthdays May 24-31
Day & Year

_____

_____

_____

_____

_____

_____

51

Sweetbrier Rose

June is the month of the rose, the symbol of romantic love. Classical Greece believed the rose was born of Cupid's smile and consecrated to Aphrodite, the goddess of love and beauty.

This week's birthday flower is the eglantine, *Rosa eglanteria,* a wild rose precious to English poets and French lovers. It grows throughout Europe and western Asia and has naturalized in eastern North America. The first rose perfume of the season is launched on spring breezes by the leaves of the plant, a fresh, clean scent that is one of the most exquisite in nature. Later, small deep pink blossoms open, releasing a delicate fragrance of their own. They are followed

in fall by flaming orange-scarlet rose hips. But beware — this beauty is a fiercely armed treasure. The thorns are hooked and unequaled in their power to stab. In the language of the flowers, the European sweetbrier stands for "I wound to heal." The American sweetbrier stands for "eloquent simplicity."

To find wild sweetbrier for a birthday bouquet, ramble through the countryside led by your nose. The scent of sweetbrier is especially strong on a cool, moist morning, in the early evening as dew falls, and after a shower. Use the leaves as greens for the bouquet. Or give a sweetbrier plant for this

birthday. Sweetbriers are sold by rose specialists and nurseries that deal in fragrant plants. If the pink of the eglantine flower doesn't appeal to you, look for the burnet rose, *Rosa spinosissima.* The flowers of the species are usually white, and the cultivars known as the Scotch roses include reds and yellows.

Wild roses are always armed with thorns: those growing on open ground have straight thorns; roses needing other plants for support have hooks that face downward.

Birthdays June 1-7
Day & Year

_____

_____

_____

_____

_____

_____

Perfume Rose

The opulent perfume roses that bloom so lavishly this month have been romantic symbols and important sources of scent for as long as people have loved good smells. Various species of these sumptuous purveyors of perfume have special meanings. *Rosa centifolia,* the "rose of a hundred petals" or cabbage rose, is the ambassador of love and a symbol of grace. *Rosa damascena,* the damask rose, is a symbol of praise for a beautiful complexion; the blooms are huge, flat-topped roses with a quartered effect. The passionate message of the French rose, *Rosa gallica,* is, "Meet me by moonlight"; the petals of its fulsome pink double form, the Apothecary rose, *Rosa gal-*

lica 'Officinalis', are even more fragrant after drying, which makes them important in potpourris and other dry perfumes.

The fragrance of the rose sets the standard for other florals. The perfumes of individual roses can vary greatly, but they have in common a rich, sweet aroma with a fruity note. Ages before Cleopatra strewed rose petals knee-deep for Anthony, the plants were domesticated and their perfumed petals were harvested. Throughout the Dark Ages, the "roser" was an important part of every monastic herb garden. Rose petals were a source of flavor, pharmaceuticals, fragrance — and of the poetic inspiration that healed the spirit.

Some of the ancient methods for collecting the

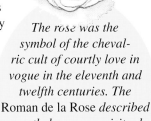

essential fragrant oils in the petals are useful today. Steam distillation of fresh petals, usually of the damask rose, produces oil of roses (attar of roses). The rose water generated by the process flavored confections from the seventeenth to the nineteenth century. Vanilla eventually replaced it, but rose water still is sold by perfumers and makes a delightful gift. Use it to flavor a whipped cream topping for the birthday cake and garnish the cake with rose petals. They are edible.

Make this birthday gift a dozen long-stemmed perfume roses; in the trade they're called "garden" roses. Include a recipe for a rose potpourri — and suggest that the petals of the bouquet become its first ingredient.

You can also give a rose plant with a romantic history, classed as Old Garden Roses in the catalogues. Among the most fragrant are Gallica 'Belle de Crécy', which opens pink and matures to soft violet; 'Souvenir de Malmaison', a quartered shell pink that still grows at Malmaison; 'Jardins de Bagatelle', an elegant pale pink; and 'Maréchal Niel', a gorgeously perfumed yellow.

The rose was the symbol of the chevalric cult of courtly love in vogue in the eleventh and twelfth centuries. The Roman de la Rose *described courtly love as a spiritual relationship in which a lover dedicated himself to his lady, expecting nothing in return.*

Birthdays June 8-15
Day & Year

_____

_____

_____

_____

_____

_____

Hybrid Tea Rose

The most popular rose in the world is the exquisitely scented hybrid tea. The fragrance has a hint of a delicate tea but more of delicious sweet ripe fruit — perhaps strawberries or apples. All the tea roses have some fragrance, especially those growing in considerable bright sun. The fragrance is stronger in flowers still on the bush than in cut roses. In the language of the flowers, this birthday flower brings the message "Your beauty is always new."

The tea rose's high-centered, urn-shaped form, pointed buds, and long flowering season are inherited from the Far Eastern roses cultivated before the Great Wall of China was built. The exquisitely scented tea rose, *Rosa odorata,* and the China rose, *Rosa chinensis,* arrived in Europe with fragrant cargoes of tea in the mid-1700s on the old China traders. Napoleon's Empress Josephine and her gardeners at Malmaison were among those who began cross-breeding the old garden roses that bloomed only in spring with the newcomers that bloomed all season. The hybrid tea, introduced in 1867, changed the world of roses. Today's hybrid teas bloom from spring into late fall, but in June they flower so lavishly, heaven seems to have come to earth.

Tea roses are harvested in nurseries that supply florists year-round. Sniff as you choose the birthday bouquet, keeping in mind that the scent will be stronger after the flower has warmed than when it comes out of the florist's chilled glass case. The florist can also order scented roses on very short notice. 'Lavonde', a lavender rose, is the most fragrant of the florist's teas; yellow 'Lovely Girl' has a fabulous scent and a bit of a blush or flame on its petals. In Texas, order yellow 'Texas Girl'. Include a note recommending that the stems be recut under water, then placed in tepid water containing floral preservative.

If the gift is for someone with a scrap of garden or even a balcony that receives six hours of sun a day, make it a fragrant hybrid tea plant. Among the most fragrant are coral-red 'Fragrant Cloud', deep pink 'Miss All-American Beauty', and 'Double Delight', a red rose with a white heart.

Birthdays June 16-23
Day & Year

_____

_____

_____

_____

_____

_____

JUNE

Miniature Rose

The scented miniature rose is an adorable little flower that reserves its scent for adventurous noses — but it's there, a floral emblem of secret strength and discreet allure. The blossoms of some miniatures have the high center and tapering form of a perfectly shaped hybrid tea. Others repeat the contours of *Rosa gallica,* which inspired the rose medallion windows in many of the great Gothic cathedrals. Many — perhaps most — miniatures are hybrids of 'Minima', a selection of the China rose, and share its marvelous summer-long blooming.

Most florists stock miniature roses for bouquets. Make your birthday bouquet unique by combining miniatures with aromatic herbs — lavender, sprigs of mint, and lemon verbena. Choose roses whose color and form speak in the language of the flowers. A red rose is always a symbol of love, and a red rosebud says, "You are pure and lovely." A white rose says, "I am worthy of you." You may want to avoid yellow roses, which are an accusation of declining love and a declaration of jealousy.

At this time of year, flower markets are filled with potted miniature rose plants that are covered with blossoms and buds. Twelve to eighteen inches high, they will bear masses of little roses until frost. For a birthday gift, sniff out a fragrant plant, or order from a specialist. Among the best for scent are 'Starina', 'Jennifer', 'Pacesetter', and 'Party Girl'.

This little flower succeeds almost anywhere as long as it gets six hours of direct sun daily. Half a dozen plants will fill a window box with color and flowers all summer. A single plant makes a charming hanging basket and will even thrive for a time inside on a sunny windowsill.

Birthdays June 24-30
Day & Year

Lavender

With its sweet, sharp, clean, and extraordinary lasting scent, this fragrant flowering herb is the shining star of dry perfumes, a miracle worker. In the language of ancient herbals, lavender is "good for all griefs," full of sunshine and sweetness, and able to "make one merry." With it our forebears fended off black magic, depression, and lethargy. A 1551 recipe promises that "lavender quilted in a cap and daily worne are good for all diseases of the head that come of a cold cause, and that they comfort the braine very well."

The aroma in the buds, stems, and needlelike foliage of this small shrub lingers for years and sweetens everything it touches. Lavender was the scent of preference for the bath in ancient Rome. Dried lavender buds and rose petals were basic ingredients in Elizabethan potpourris and sachets. Sheaves of lavender were strewn on cottage floors, in Gypsy caravans, and before monarchs at coronation ceremonies. Fragrant geranium leaves, verbena, and lavender filled the "sweet bags" hung on furniture to perfume musty rooms. Lavender is still the preferred scent for linens — sleep comes sweeter in lavendered sheets — and we still use it to flavor fancy honey, conserves, and the magical seasoning known as Herbes de Provence.

Lavender blooms in late June and July and often repeats in September. Florists stock, or can order, stems of fresh lavender at this season. Garnish the frosting on the birthday cake with a few lavender buds, and combine lavender stems and small white roses with lots of lavender-colored ribbon to make a birthday bouquet.

A gardener always has room for one more pot of lavender. You'll find potted plants and flats of seedlings at garden markets. A good gift for the new gardener is a set of seedlings to complete an herb garden — English lavender, French thyme, rosemary, Greek oregano, marjoram, hyssop, parsley, dill, sage, and bergamot, which bees love.

When you are buying a lavender plant, look for silvery English lavender, a Mediterranean native that is best for fragrance, *Lavandula angustifolia* subspecies *angustifolia.* It's also known as *Lavandula vera,* true lavender, and *Lavandula officinalis.* Spanish or French lavender, *Lavandula stoechas,* is a better choice for a garden in a hot region and for an indoor plant.

Birthdays July 1-7
Day & Year

_____

_____

_____

_____

_____

_____

For drying, harvest stems of lavender just before the buds open. Save lavender clippings to throw on the fire; heat releases its heavenly aroma.

Magnolia

The first sight of an evergreen magnolia coming into bloom in late June or July is breathtaking. The flower is majestic, a cream-white primitive that floats like a water lily above layers of large, stiff, lustrous dark green leaves with colorful reverses in silver, beige-brown, or rust. The fragrance is better than perfume, a blend of lily, gardenia, citrus, and ripe cantaloupe. Later, gorgeous cone-shaped coral or red-tinted fruits develop; if the stems are placed in water, the cones open and drop beautiful scarlet seeds out on threads.

This birthday blossom is the oldest flower of all. Long before roses or chrysanthemums, magnolias perfumed North America.

Fossils show that before the ice ages, evergreen magnolias were distributed over the continent. To the Europeans who settled America, these magnificent trees were symbols of high-minded aspirations.

Magnolia foliage is sold all year long, and the blossoms of sweet and bull bay magnolias can be ordered through florists. Or you may find one in a neighboring tree — magnolias grow from southern Massachusetts to Florida and west to California. An arrangement of one flower and a few leaves makes an elegant birthday centerpiece. Press the stem into wet foam and surround the flower with the leaves arranged to show the color of the reverse sides.

_____

_____

_____

_____

_____

A magnolia tree for the garden makes a sumptuous birthday gift. Choose a good-sized seedling at a nursery. Magnolias take years to come into bloom. For a small space, the sweet bay, *Magnolia virginiana,* is best. Some years it blooms as early as May or June and often continues into September.

The bull bay is the southern or plantation *Magnolia grandiflora* and is suited only to a large landscape. The huge saucerlike flowers begin to open in May or June and must be seen to be believed! 'Little Gem' is a smaller cultivar that blooms from June until fall.

Honeysuckle

This birthday flower is the lover's vine, the twining woodbine of old English poetry and romantic literature. It symbolizes faithful love and a sweet disposition. The perfume is gentle, rising with the cool mists of morning; it is intensified at twilight and most pervasive after a soft rain. As sweet as heliotrope and sweet violet, honeysuckle once perfumed candles, tussiemussies, and nosegays. Deep inside the cream or golden flowers are drops of nectar, which draw bees and butterflies and are sweet to the tongue. Small red or black fruits attractive to birds come later.

The honeysuckle tribe, *Lonicera,* grows wild all over the Northern Hemisphere, eager to per-

fume the world. Birds love the seeds, so honeysuckle travels wherever the birds go, from the garden to neighboring forests and open lands. Soon its dainty, pointed green leaves canopy the trees, and the blossoms fill the summer air with a scent as sweet as candy.

You'll find sprays of sweetly scented honeysuckle all summer at flower shops and farmers' markets. Honeysuckle, hot pink and gold zinnias, and snapdragons make a fresh, summery birthday bouquet. Full-flowered sprigs of honeysuckle make charming, scented supports for place cards: poke the stems into flower vials to keep the sprigs fresh. If you want to give a honeysuckle plant, choose a

conservative variety. One that contains its exuberance is the beautiful Canadian cultivar *Lonicera X heckrottii* 'Goldflame'. From June to September it covers itself with tiers of carmine buds that open to yellow, then blush pink. 'Goldflame's' unsuspected treasure is an opulent nighttime fragrance comparable to that of auratum lilies, with a hint of orange and jasmine. The perfume is most intoxicating in warm regions.

In the South, winter honeysuckle, *Lonicera fragrantissima,* releases an extravagant perfume from late winter to very early spring. It is one of the world's most fragrant plants.

65

JULY

Phlox

Peace and harmony are the gifts of this birthday flower, a symbol of beauty that is essential and irreplaceable. In billows of cerise, white, pink, blue, mauve, lavender, and white, phlox occupy the middle ground of sunny gardens from now until cold weather. The most luscious pastels of mid- and late summer appear in these descendants of the native American phlox. Early settlers found them blooming in pink and lavender along stream banks, on hillsides, and at the edge of tall woodlands. British plant hunters were enchanted by the soft lavender and magenta tones and in the early 1700s shipped them home to be tamed. A mecca to bees and butterflies, the light, musty scent of phlox is the aroma of summer in the country. Warmly sweet through midsummer nights, phlox has an unmistakable, unforgettable bouquet.

For the birthday week, and many weeks to come, you'll find sedate florists' phlox by the armful at flower shops and colorful mixed bouquets of garden phlox at farmers' markets. Do something different for a birthday gift. Make an authentic Elizabethan nosegay by

binding together with satin ribbon short stems of phlox, lavender, small roses, thyme, marigolds, and bergamot.

For a gardener, seedlings of the perennial phlox, *Phlox paniculata,* are always welcome gifts. Planted now, they'll

bloom next July, and on and on. There's always space for a few more white flowers in a garden, especially 'White Admiral', 'Prime Minister,' and the mildew-resistant 'Miss Lingard'. Include on your birthday card a suggestion that the phlox would be wonderful next to lemon yellow daylilies and fabulous in a patio planter with rubrum lilies.

You should mention that phlox must be deadheaded as soon as the blossoms fade; otherwise, next summer these madly generous plants will choke your whites with magenta seedlings.

Birthdays July 24-31
Day & Year

_____

_____

_____

_____

_____

_____

The color of blue phlox holds up better in a little shade.

Oriental Lily

The aristocratic Oriental lily is a tall, flamboyant beauty whose perfume is simply extraordinary. Rich as heavy cream, silky as fine skin, not quite of this world, the fragrance embraces jasmine and orange blossoms, myrrh, spice, and something more. In mid- and late summer the Oriental's regal stalks are spangled with eight to ten or twenty huge lilies. The colors range from sparkling white to pearly pink, crimson, and crimson blushed pink. Many varieties are banded or rayed with gold and splashed or speckled with vermilion.

This magnificent birthday flower is a hybrid of the twentieth century, one that mingles the characteristics of four exquisite Japanese lilies. The Oriental's gold is from the gold-band lily, *Lilium auratum* var. *platyphyllum.* Introduced in 1861, this is Mam-yuri, the lily that grows wild on the slopes of Mount Fuji. The Oriental's reflexed and twisted petals and the crimson flecks and pinks and reds are from *Lilium speciosum. Lilium rubellum* and the Japanese lily, *Lilium japonicum,* impart lustrous pinks and perfume.

A birthday gives you an excuse to splurge on top-quality Oriental lilies at a good florist's. One of the most beautiful lilies is 'Imperial Silver', a huge luminous white flower with vermilion dotting. With pink snapdragons, crimson stock, blue delphinium, and summer lilac, it makes a magnificent bouquet.

When you buy lilies, select flowers that have one or two open blossoms, no more, and whose lower buds show some color. They'll last longer and stay fresh if you strip away the bottom leaves, recut the stems, and place them in warm water containing floral preservative. Lily

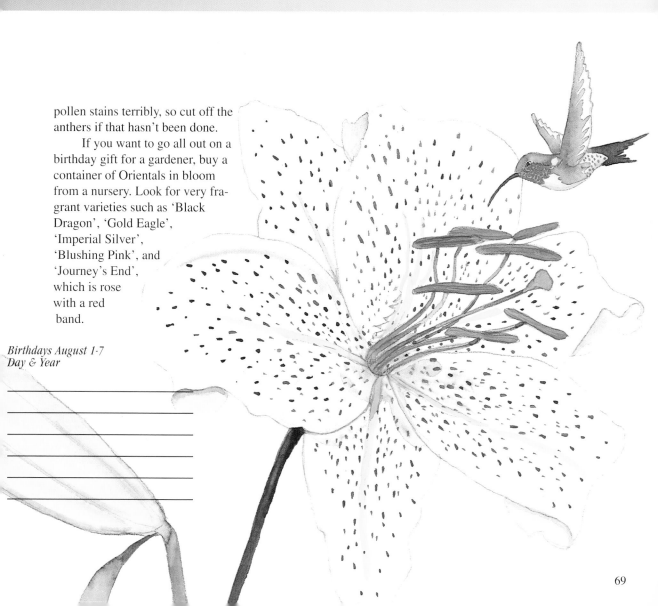

pollen stains terribly, so cut off the anthers if that hasn't been done.

If you want to go all out on a birthday gift for a gardener, buy a container of Orientals in bloom from a nursery. Look for very fragrant varieties such as 'Black Dragon', 'Gold Eagle', 'Imperial Silver', 'Blushing Pink', and 'Journey's End', which is rose with a red band.

Birthdays August 1-7
Day & Year

_____

_____

_____

_____

_____

_____

Stock

This week celebrates the blossom the Elizabethans called stock-gilliflower for the aroma of clove that dominates its fragrance. Stock came to the West long ago from southern Europe and is associated with love. In a fifteenth-century manuscript called *Livre du Cuer d'Amours* (*Book from the Heart of Love* or *From the Loving Heart*), stock appears in an exquisite little painting of a "pleasure" garden. It is shown edging a grassy lawn in a border with the most valued flowers and herbs of the period — roses, carnations, pinks, columbine, mallow, and rosemary.

Two species of stock are common. The beautiful day-blooming stock, *Matthiola incana,* is a florist's summer and fall staple. The flowering stems are tall and heavily encrusted with small multipetaled blossoms in rich pastels. Lovely as larkspur, warmly perfumed, the gilliflower is a symbol of lasting beauty in the courtly language of the flowers.

The other species, *Matthiola longipetala,* is an annual called evening stock and perfume plant. Its broad-petaled pale lilac flowers open at dusk to release a wondrous essence of sweet cloves, lilies, and exotic spices. Though evening stock is dull by day, its perfume rises heavy and sweet on the cool night air — an enchantment not to be resisted, never to be forgotten.

You'll have no trouble finding day-blooming stock for a birthday bouquet. With Iceland poppies, a large red rose, and baby's breath, stock makes a lovely bouquet. Select stems on which half to two thirds of the lower blossoms are open.

Evening stock is a more precious gift because you'll probably need

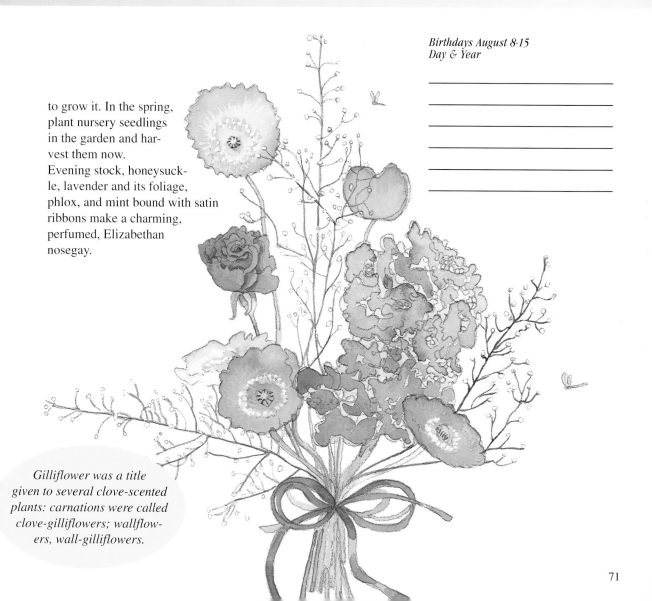

to grow it. In the spring, plant nursery seedlings in the garden and harvest them now.

Evening stock, honeysuckle, lavender and its foliage, phlox, and mint bound with satin ribbons make a charming, perfumed, Elizabethan nosegay.

Gilliflower was a title given to several clove-scented plants: carnations were called clove-gilliflowers; wallflowers, wall-gilliflowers.

Spider Lily

The exotic, exquisite, and extravagantly fragrant spider lily, *Hymenocallis narcissiflora* or Peruvian daffodil, is a native of valleys and steep slopes in the Peruvian and Bolivian Andes, a work of art put up by a large bulb. First, a two-foot-tall fleshy stalk rises. Then two to five large buds clustered at the top of the stem begin to open in a sequence that recalls the blooming of its relative, the amaryllis. The lilies are like huge, glowing white or golden daffodils backed by halos of narrow, reflexed white petals. Up close, the perfume is powerful — think of the sweet, satiny, lemon-jasmine of a paperwhite narcissus. The polished outward-arching strap leaves are dark green and stay handsome long after the flowers go by.

In warm regions, the spider lily is a familiar summer bedding plant that requires little care and comes back faithfully every year. In cooler regions, it is grown in a container. Set out in early summer, it comes into bloom about now. When cold weather is approaching, the bulb is lifted and stored indoors for the winter.

For this birthday, order a stem or two of spider lily from a florist. Tied with wide white satin ribbon and presented in a long florist's box, they will make an elegant and unusual gift.

Or give a potful of spider lilies in bloom. Nurseries and mail order catalogues sell the bulbs. In early summer, plant two or three in a decorative pot and grow them in good light on a patio or a balcony. With luck, they'll bloom this week.

You can also be madly extravagant and give a season-long display of spider lilies. First, a Peruvian daffodil. Then *Hymenocallis liriosme,* a water-loving species that flowers from late spring to midsummer. Finally there's *Hymenocallis speciosa,* known as winter spice in the West Indies, which blooms indoors in the fall.

Birthdays August 16-23
Day & Year

_____

_____

_____

_____

_____

_____

Tuberose

Pearly white, dainty, exquisitely fragrant, the tuberose represents dangerous pleasures in the language of the flowers. If perfume could be addictive, then the tuberose would really be dangerous. The scent is silky, sweet, rich, something like jasmine, but deep-toned. It is released by spikes of many-petaled tubular flowers that bloom on a tall, slim stem above grassy foliage. Double-flowered tuberoses are the most beautiful, but the perfume of the single-flowered varieties is unequaled.

Tuberoses have been cultivated for centuries in southern France, the United States, and Africa for use in the perfume industry and to provide cut flowers for florists. Tuberoses are still used in perfumery because their scent can't be replicated synthetically. The blossoms continue to produce perfume even after the flower has been picked — a rare and immensely valuable characteristic.

The origin of the tuberose, *Polianthes tuberosa,* is something of a mystery, for it has never been found growing in the wild. In the early 1600s, a Parisian botanist and apothecary named Jean Robin made this Mexican import fashionable. Robin was the director of the Louvre gardens under three kings and raised plants on the Ile de la Cité for his patrons. News of the fabulous new fragrance plant appeared in his influential plant catalogue, one of the first ever published. The popularity of the tuberose continued into the Victorian era, and it was a star in the all-white "moon gardens" much loved at the time.

Florists carry tuberose in season and will order it for you. For

an elegant birthday bouquet, bind tuberoses, large shell pink roses, and asparagus fern with narrow silver and rose-pink ribbons.

Or grow them yourself. It's not difficult. In April, pot tuberose corms and keep them on a partly sunny sill until June. Then move them outdoors. If all goes well, they'll bloom plentifully enough to supply a birthday bouquet.

Birthdays August 24-31
Day & Year

_____
_____
_____
_____
_____
_____

Frangipani

A gorgeous tropical beauty, frangipani, *Plumeria rubra,* is chief among flowers in a lei, a hula dancer's perfumed festival garland. The blossom is a flat cluster of overlapping florets with a few unopened buds peeping through; it's so much like a nosegay that the tree is called the nosegay tree. Frangipani's colors range from cool white to intense shades of gold, rose, salmon, and red, and there are sumptuous combinations. The flowers have short stems and, once cut, last only for a day or so. On the tree, frangipani remains beautiful for an astonishing twenty or thirty days.

This birthday flower's beauty is enhanced by an exotic fragrance with a history. It seems the original frangipani scent was developed to perfume leather cured in a tannery owned by a noble Roman family named Frangipane. When *Plumeria rubra* was discovered in tropical America in the 1600s, the scent was likened to frangipani and the name clung. The original

scent must have been sweet and spicy, judging by modern hybrids. Jasmine and spice are there, with various fruity overtones — citrus, coconut, honeysuckle, rose, raspberry, peach, apricot, carnation.

Plumeria is in bloom now from Hawaii to Texas and even in Canada. In cool regions, it is grown as a container plant that summers outdoors in full sun and spends winter indoors. At 38 degrees Fahrenheit, plumeria looses its bold foliage and looks dead as a stick. Its return to life in spring seems so miraculous that frangipani has been associated with immortality by some Eastern religions.

The florist's plumeria is an expensive import from Hawaii or the South Seas. It is used in fabulous bridal corsages and centerpieces and makes a great, if short-lived, birthday gift. A potted plumeria in bloom is something else, and you can raise it yourself. Plumeria planted in late spring should be in bloom this week. You can order plumeria cuttings, which almost root themselves in spring, through the suppliers listed in Barton's *Gardening by Mail.*

Birthdays September 1-7
Day & Year

_____

_____

_____

_____

_____

Ginger Lily

The fragrance of this exquisitely intricate flower is as mellow as a ripe tangerine, as sweet as honeysuckle in full bloom — light by day, intoxicating at night. An exotic found in the Himalayas, China, and India, *Hedychium* flowers from midsummer to autumn on a sturdy stalk, four to seven feet tall, that looks like a corn plant married to a canna. Each bulb bears one stem layered with broad leaves and topped by a large flowerhead composed of many overlapping bracts. Each bract produces a very fragrant, mothlike blossom with long, spidery filaments. The flowering goes on for several weeks as the blooms fade and others open to take their place.

The ginger lily has naturalized in the rain forest of Puerto Rico and elsewhere in the tropical Americas. It's well known on estate gardens in the South, where it colonizes in the partial shade of tall trees. At the end of the growing season on the Gulf Coast, *Hedychium* stems are cut into two- and three-leaf sections to use as greens in large flower arrangements. In cool regions the bulb is handled like canna — planted in spring in the garden or in a container, then dug out in autumn and stored indoors.

Florists sell ginger lilies by the stem this time of year. With yellow cosmos, zinnias, and the big, bold gold-flecked foliage of aucuba, a ginger lily makes a handsome birthday bouquet.

Or give a potful of assorted ginger lilies. The most fragrant is white *Hedychium coronarium,* which is known by a convoy of common names — garland flower, butterfly ginger, white ginger, butterfly lily, and cinnamon jasmine. *Hedychium flavum* is smaller, a delicately scented yellow ginger lily used in leis in the Pacific islands. *Hedychium gardneranum,* the kahili ginger lily of Hawaiian gardens, bears yellow flowers with long red filaments on a long spike. *Hedychium ellipticum* combines white florets, red filaments, and golden stems.

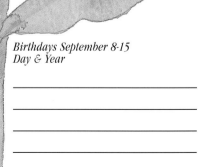

Birthdays September 8-15
Day & Year

_____

_____

_____

_____

_____

_____

Belladonna Lily

The beautiful lady lily opens imperious rosy pink silk trumpets on a tall, slim stalk and fills late summer with the fragrance of sugar and spice — part lily-of-the-valley and part fresh cinnamon buns. In each cluster, there are two and more often four narrow, lilylike trumpets. The usual color is a luscious rosy pink, but rose-red and rose-white are common. *Amaryllis belladonna,* its botanical name, means beautiful lady amaryllis, but it is known by another common name, naked ladies. In the beginning of summer the bulb sends up a fountain of broad blue-green leaves, which subside. Then a naked eighteen- to twenty-four-inch stalk rises, fully justifying the common name. To soften the starkness, mums, hostas, and other low-growing species are planted at its feet, and the beautiful lady lily emerges.

This birthday flower is a true amaryllis but more charming than the amaryllis (*Hippeastrum*) that blooms indoors in winter. A big bulb native to Southwest Africa, the belladonna lily is a common bedding flower in frost-free regions. Given winter protection, it becomes a perennial as far north as Zone 7. Farther north, the bulb is replanted in late spring and taken indoors in the fall.

The belladonna lily is available as a cut flower in summer and fall. For an extravagant birthday bouquet, combine belladonna lilies, blue delphinium, salvia or perovskia, white phlox, and cascades of small-leaved ivy. Recut the lily stems and stand them in deep water for several hours before arranging them in water containing a floral preservative.

Another possibility is to give a potful of belladonna lilies with soft fuzzy things growing at their feet — variegated ivy, pansies, dwarf heather, scented geraniums, or coleus. In spring you'll find bulbs for sale in garden centers and catalogues.

Birthdays September 16-22
Day & Year

_____

_____

_____

_____

_____

Heliotrope

A joint French and Spanish plant expedition found *Heliotropium arborescens* in Peru in the 1700s, and the pervasive sweetness of the scent quickly established heliotrope as a favorite of perfumers and florists. The Victorians and Edwardians, in their rich, rustling purple silks and violet satins, were wearing the colors of a favorite perfume, heliotrope. By the 1920s and 1930s it had become a literary symbol used by authors such as Colette to signal romantic nostalgia.

The plant is a little woody subshrub whose pretty, crinkled dark green leaves compete for attention with fluffy clusters of florets. The blossoms are a deep lavender-blue when they open; as they mature, they pale to violet, then violet-white. White varieties are very sweetly scented. In the garden, heliotrope is not showy, but if you pass the plant on a warm summer evening the fragrance of even a few blossoms will make you pause. It fills the air with a delicious and indescribably sweet, soft scent, something like the sweet vanilla smell of good pastry. There's a haunting undertone, a touch of old damask rose or honeysuckle. Heliotrope's nickname is cherry pie!

Heliotrope planted in the spring blooms until the high heat, then comes back with the fall rain to perfume Indian summer. The best plants are sold in the fall and make delightful birthday gifts. Choose heliotrope for

_____

_____

_____

_____

_____

_____

its perfume, not its color. Wrap the pot in lavender paper and poke a purple satin bow down into the foliage. Or repot the plant in a hanging basket with cerise verbena and white petunias.

With the gift include a note suggesting that the plant start life in the garden and come indoors when the cold weather arrives. It will continue to bloom on a sun-drenched sill. Its name indicates a plant that turns its flowers or leaves to receive the most sunlight.

When heliotrope is just full of fragrant blossoms, harvest the crop, break the blooms into sprigs, and dry them to scent a pot-pourri.

83

Mums

The chrysanthemum is the floral emblem of autumn — fall's earth-toned rainbow, its pungent, piney aroma. It was cultivated in China at least five hundred years before Christ was born, and in the mystical Chinese garden tradition linking spiritual oneness and the contemplation of nature, the late-flowering chrysanthemum was the symbol of longevity — beautiful forever. Orchids, bamboos, chrysanthemums, and flowering plums represented the four seasons of the year as well as ideal human qualities — grace, dependability, resilience, nobility, courage, and endurance.

In Japan the chrysanthemum was adopted as the personal emblem of the emperor in 1797. On the imperial flag it was represented as a disk surrounded by sixteen petals, now simplified to a naked disk. In the early nineteenth century, seventy varieties of mums were introduced in Europe and swept the horticultural world. In those days they bloomed only in autumn, as the days grew shorter. Techniques developed in this century bring garden mums into bloom year-round, and mums now rank with roses in commercial importance. The longevity of the cut flower rivals that of the carnation and has made a place for it in all florists' arrangements.

This week's birthday flower is an exotic mum. There are several: the gorgeous multicolored football mum, the eccentric spider mum, and the bright little button mum. One stem of each, with burgundy-red oak leaves and berried branches, make a spectacular birthday bouquet. Choose the colors carefully: in the language of the flowers a red mum says, "I love you"; a yellow mum complains of

The blossoms of florists' mums stay fresh longer in water containing floral preservative, but the leaves will turn yellow.

slighted love; a white mum stands for truth.

A potted mum makes a wonderfully aromatic birthday present, and there are dozens of colors to choose from: gold, mauve, pink, white, maroon, red, and their variations.

Gardenia

A beautiful cream-white velvet rose set against glossy emerald-green leaves — that's a gardenia. Its perfume is as thrilling as jasmine and as sweet as orange blossoms, but richer. The fragrance of this fabulous flower catches your awareness as soon as it begins to open on the shrub, and even when the flower is fading, up close the perfume remains noticeable.

Gardenia jasminoides is a big, handsome evergreen shrub that came to the West from China in the mid-1700s. It is known as the Cape jasmine for its jasminelike scent and because it was first thought that the plant came from the Cape of Good Hope. The large-flowered double variety, *Gardenia jasminoides* 'Fortuniana', is the florist's gardenia. It was named for Robert Fortune, who conducted plant explorations in China for the Royal Horticultural Society. In gardens in the South, in Mexico, and in tropical America, the shrub blooms in late spring and summer. In greenhouses in the North, where it has been grown since colonial times, it comes into bloom later. Victorian debutantes dreamed of receiving a snowy gardenia from the hands of an admirer in top hat and tails. Perfumers dreamed of extracting its essential oils to make perfume. Many debutantes got their wish; the perfumers did not.

A gardenia from the florist is a gorgeous birthday present and needs nothing to enhance its beauty.

For the indoor gardener with a sunny windowsill, a delightful gift is the wonderful little fall- and win-

_____
_____
_____
_____
_____
_____

ter-blooming gardenia called
'Prostrata'. The plants begin to appear
at garden markets and florists now.
Before you wrap your gift, set it on a
plant saucer filled with pebbles. In the
card explain that with the sustained
humidity provided by moist pebbles,
with acid fertilizer, and with summers
outdoors, it could bloom for a lifetime.

A thin mulch of coffee grounds is the secret of success with a windowsill gardenia.

Jasmine

Jasmine is one of the great ancient perfume flowers, a small blossom with a glorious past. In the gardens of Persia it bloomed with the perfume plants — narcissus, lilac, orange trees, roses — among cool pavilions, fountains, fruit trees, and birdsong. There was jasmine in the paradise garden that the followers of Islam created centuries later to represent the state of blessedness promised to its faithful. In the "adorations" painted by the masters, jasmine was a symbol of the star-spangled heavens from which the Christ Child descended. Jasmine bushes still line the entrances of certain Hindu temples and play a part in religious ceremonies.

The principal jasmine species are shrubs, or climbers, native to India and Persia, which bloom now and off and on during the year. The flowers are dainty and starlike — white usually, or blushed rosy pink — and artless. But just a few blossoms will perfume the surrounding air. Its fragrance has the richness of hyacinths and the sweetness of lily-of-the-valley. Yet it is so unique that chemists must include drops of oil of jasmine in the synthetic perfumes that seek to imitate it. Next to the tuberose, jasmine is the most expensive floral oil. Like the tuberose, jasmine produces perfume even after it has been cut, a rare and valuable characteristic.

You may not find jasmine at the florist's, but you can order it. A very special gift for this birthday is a nosegay of sprigs of scented jasmine combined with a big pink rose and tied with pink satin ribbon.

For the indoor gardener, a fabulous present is a basketful of jasmine plants chosen to provide a year-long sequence of fragrance: *Jasminum sambac* blooms now and again in spring and summer; the many-petaled star jasmine, *Jasminum nitidum,* blooms intermittently; poet's jessamine, *Jasminum officinale,* blooms indoors in winter, and has the most heavenly perfume; the famous French perfume jasmine, *Jasminum officinale* var. *grandiflorum,* blooms in early spring; and the winter jasmine, *Jasminum polyanthum,* blooms around Valentine's Day.

Birthdays October 16-23
Day & Year

_____

_____

_____

_____

_____

_____

Jesemain Water
*Take two handfuls of
Jeseme flowers and put them
in a flagon or earthen pot, put to
them about a quart of fair water
and a quarter pound of Sugar, let
this stand and steep about half an
hour, then take your water and flowers and pour them out of one vessel
into another until such time the
water hath taken on the sent and
taste of the flowers.*
— A recipe from one of the mas-
ter cooks to Charles II,
1682

Cattleya Orchid

As breathtaking as an exotic butterfly, the fragrant *Cattleya* is a beautiful tropical orchid whose form we associate with corsages. Most cattleyas have some scent, but the one designated for this birthday week pours out currents of sweetness that draw you irresistibly to it at any fall orchid display. Musky, citrusy, or sweet, the fragrance is rich, complex, and different in each variety.

The cattleyas are native to the mountains and foothills of northern South America. The pseudobulbs live perched precariously in trees with their roots dangling in the air. They prefer temperatures between 60 and 80 degrees Fahrenheit and thrive on seasons of rain that alternate with dry periods. The first orchids to arrive in Europe were shipped in the mid-1700s from the Bahamas to England. Efforts to grow orchids there failed until the glass house (greenhouse) was developed. In its controlled climate, the cultivation, reproduction, and hybridization of tropical orchids became possible. Like other orchids, cattleya blossoms that remain undisturbed on the plant are very long-lived: cut, they stay fresh for at least a week and as long as four weeks.

This week's birthday gift presents no challenge at all. Florists carry cattleyas, and they make beautiful corsages and centerpieces.

Florists, nurseries, and mail order specialists also carry cattleya plants, which bloom easily enough in an east or west window. Among truly fragrant orchids available from specialists are 'Beau Bells', a lovely old white cattleya

whose perfume is a silky lily-of-the-valley smell-alike; laeliocattleya 'Socrates', a large purple cross between a laelia species and a cattleya, with an incomparable sweetness; Chit Chat 'Tangerine', with clusters of fragrant bright orange flowers; cattleya 'Cover Girl' and the brassolaeliocattleya 'Killarney', green with magenta or purple lips, with a heavenly fragrance of orange or lime; BLC 'Misty Lime', all green, with the aroma of a sweet ripe lime.

An orchid is shipped with its stem immersed in a vial of water. Recut the stem, place it in fresh water, and keep it in a cool place at night. It will last a week.

Birthdays October 24-31
Day & Year

_____

_____

_____

_____

_____

_____

Bouvardia

With its pretty silken blossoms and delicious jasminelike fragrance, long-lived bouvardia lights up the gray end of the year. *Bouvardia longiflora,* the white flower known in Mexico as *flores de San Juan,* is a perfumed species whose scent is extraordinary, particularly at night.

Bouvardia's showy clusters of tubular flowers bloom in both fall and winter on small shrubs native to Mexico and Central America. The cultivated bouvardias are nearly all hybrids, descendants of the first crosses made at Parsons Nursery, in Brighton, England, about 1857. In a solution of floral preservative, bouvardia can last as long as three weeks, which very quickly made it popular with florists. Many white, pink, and red hybrids have been developed — but the whites are still the most fragrant.

Bouvardia is available in flower shops at this season and off and on during the year. A few stems of fragrant white bouvardia with pink snapdragons, purple statice, and lemon grass for greens make a handsome birthday bouquet. To help the bouvardia to last, strip away the foliage and the shoots developing outside the blossom. Recut the stems and place them for two hours in warm water containing a few drops of lemon juice. With your gift card, include a suggestion that the bouquet be placed in water containing a floral preservative.

For the indoor gardener, a potted bouvardia is a handsome birthday gift. Choose *Bouvardia longiflora.* It will produce bursts of wonderfully fragrant flowers through Thanksgiving and well into winter. *Bouvardia ternifolia* is a smaller species that bears pretty scarlet or pink flowers, but it's not usually very fragrant.

Birthdays November 1-7
Day & Year

_____

_____

_____

_____

_____

_____

Amazon Lily

Grace and radiance — and a perfume that bewitches the senses — belong to the Amazon lily. A real beauty, it is more richly fragrant than almost any other winter plant. The luminous white clusters of *Eucharis amazonica* mingle jasmine and orange blossoms, myrrh, and Eastern spices. An exotic tropical from the high mountains of Peru and Colombia, this birthday blossom looks like a large, short-cup glistening white daffodil touched inside with gold or green. The flower develops from a bulb, like its relative the amaryllis. The buds are clustered at the top of a two-foot stalk that rises after the broad, shiny leaves have developed. Each stem bears three to six buds, which open one or two at a time to pour forth their sweet perfume.

In shaded tropical gardens, the Amazon lily is used as a bedding plant; it blooms two or three times a year with dry periods of rest in between. In the North, it is grown in warm greenhouses and as a pot plant on sunny patios and windowsills. Bloom times are not entirely predictable, but bulbs planted in late summer flower about now. With luck, they'll bloom again in winter and spring.

For your birthday gift, ask the florist to order an Amazon lily and to combine it with baby's-breath and smilax. Have it tied with a satin rib-

Birthdays November 8-15
Day & Year

_____

_____

_____

_____

_____

_____

bon to make a fragrant nosegay.

Or grow this gift yourself. You'll find bulbs at garden centers and in mail order catalogues. In late August, plant the bulb in a five-inch pot with its tip at soil level. Keep it outdoors in the shade until it sprouts, then move it indoors and bring it into bloom in a sunny window.

The secret to success with an Amazon lily to keep the roots potbound. Never disturb them.

95

Fragrant Glory-bower

The blossom of the fragrant glory-bower *Clerodendrum philippinum* looks like a little nosegay of peach-white or pink-white one-inch double roses backed by big hydrangea leaves. The perfume is like that of the gold-band lily or a fine jasmine, soft with a hint of an exotic Eastern spice. The species is a big, bushy, sun-loving evergreen shrub that blooms from late winter through Christmas in Florida landscapes and in the tropical climates where it has naturalized. In the North, the fragrant glory-bower is a conservatory plant and a shrub for the indoor garden. There it flowers from summer through November, and on.

This species first appeared in the West in the middle of the last century, an import from China and Japan. The exotic note in the fragrance earned it the common name of Cashmere-bouquet. Cashmere, or Kashmir, a former princely state bordered by India, Pakistan, and China, is a land of high mountains and ancient rivers, famous as a land of mystery and beauty since Mogul times. Some colorful clerodendrums came later from Africa, but none can match Cashmere-bouquet for fragrance.

Not all garden centers carry Cashmere-bouquet. For this week's birthday gift, you will probably have to look to mail order specialists such as Logee's Greenhouses in Danielson, Connecticut. Garden markets carry clerodendrums, among them a new hanging basket form that flowers all year long. It's a hybrid of *C. philippinum* and should have some of the original perfume. On your birthday card, include a note recommending summers in the sun for your gift.

Birthdays November 16-23
Day & Year

_____

_____

_____

_____

_____

_____

Carolina Jasmine

 This birthday flower covers itself with golden blossoms that fill the air with a jasminelike perfume, rich as hyacinths, sweet as violets. The scent is modest when the plant first comes into bloom and grows stronger as the season advances and more and more flowers appear. The blossoms are tubular, ending in small, charming rosettes that shower with gold the plant's profusion of shiny green leaves and handsome mahogany stems.

Gelsimium sempervirens is the horticultural name for this very good-looking twining climber native to the southeastern United States. It grows wild by the edges of woodlands from Virginia southward, west to Texas, and down into Central America. *Sempervirens* means evergreen, and at the warm end of its range Carolina jasmine does become evergreen or partly evergreen. Bloom times are according to the climate. In gardens in the South, it flowers from winter to midspring. On potted plants in greenhouses and indoor gardens, the buds begin to swell after a period of cold in the fall and will go on flowering intermittently for several months.

To make a charming and different birthday gift, buy a small Carolina jasmine plant, five small yellow roses, a decorative hanging basket, and five flower vials (found at craft stores). Repot the jasmine in the hanging basket, fill the vials with water containing a floral preservative, and push them down into the soil around the plant; place the roses in the vials and add a big yellow satin bow.

In your birthday note, include a warning that the flowers and parts of the plant are poisonous.

Birthdays November 24-30
Day & Year

_____

_____

_____

_____

_____

_____

DECEMBER

Scented Cyclamen

A potful of color is this flower's gift to the last month of the year — color, and a light sweet scent that is a bit musky and has a hint of freesia. A cyclamen in bloom is exceptionally showy because the flowers stand well above the gorgeous silver-splashed leaves and open dozens at a time. The buds keep popping up and opening, and the flowers remain fresh for a week or ten days. Cyclamen comes in luminous white, vibrant scarlet, pink, salmon, red, and lavender. There are also bicolors. A white cyclamen often has a red or a purple mouth, and the petals of some whites are splashed with purple or crimson. The flower looks like a shooting star on a sinuous golden brown stalk or perhaps a sky diver, chute swept

back, face down, mouth open, and splashed a deeper red or a brighter pink. When the blossom falls, its stalk coils inward and curves down to deposit the seedhead on the soil. Southeastern Europe and Asia Minor are the home of the cyclamen, whose blooming season runs from November to April.

For an elegant birthday plant that will bloom all winter and on into spring, choose a cyclamen. If you want to give a fabulous but moderately priced gift, fill a plant tray the length of a windowsill with pots of cyclamens in various colors. You'll find cyclamens in the flower markets in the fall and through the winter. Let your nose choose the plant.

The inch-long miniatures of the European cyclamen, *Cyclamen purpurascens* (*Cyclamen europaeum*), tend to be the most fragrant.

The blooms may be white with a scarlet mouth, lavender, salmon, or shades of rosy red. It's harder to find scented varieties of the beautiful large-flowered Persian cyclamen, but they exist. The scarlet 'Renown' is fragrant.

On your card, suggest planting the cyclamen in the garden when it stops blooming. In partial shade, watered through droughts, a cyclamen usually maintains its lovely foliage and may throw a few blooms in the fall.

A just-opened cyclamen blossom in a bud vase will stay fresh for at least a week. With a few leaves from the plant, it makes a pretty little bouquet.

Birthdays December 1-7
Day & Year

_____

_____

_____

_____

_____

_____

Winter Daphne

Daphne odora, winter daphne, is an attractive, low, slow-growing evergreen that is reputed to be the most fragrant shrub in the world. The blossom is a terminal nosegay of pink or purple buds that open to little creamy white flowers and pour out an amazing perfume. The fragrance is ambrosia — sunshine on a sweet orange tree with hints of coconut and spice or perhaps basil. A potted plant will bloom by a cool sunny windowsill and in a greenhouse in December and January. In gardens in the mild Northwest and in the South, daphnes come into bloom later in winter.

Its famous fragrance is winter daphne's crowning glory, but beautiful foliage is its year-round asset. The leaves are shiny and look very much like long, narrow, and elegant versions of the leaves of a bay laurel tree. That similarity accounts for its name. In Greek mythology, Daphne was the personification of the laurel, a tree associated with Apollo. According to legend, this beautiful daughter of a river god rejected every lover, even Apollo. When the god pursued Daphne, her father transformed her into a laurel tree. The god appropriated the laurel for poets, and Rome later chose it to crown victors.

The first winter daphnes in the West were shipped from China in 1770 to Kew Gardens in England. Things Chinese were very much in vogue then, and before long daphne was perfuming cold, drafty Victorian parlors, where the climate felt like home.

Florists can order winter daphne for you, but not many stock it regularly. A swag of winter daphne and long-stemmed pink roses tied with lots of pink curling ribbon makes a fabulous centerpiece for a birthday buffet table.

Plants of *Daphne odora,* and of a pretty variety whose leaves are edged with gold, are easy to locate and make fine gifts for gardeners. Garden centers generally stock daphne, and it is listed in mail order catalogues.

Birthdays December 8-15
Day & Year

_____

_____

_____

_____

_____

_____

Paperwhite Narcissus

The paperwhite narcissus is a beautiful white short-cup daffodil that pours out an astonishing perfume — penetrating, musky, fruity, and fabulous. The fragrance of the double-flowered varieties is especially beautiful, rather like a fruity jasmine. The gorgeous aroma comes from a cluster of immaculate little blossoms that top a slim stem flanked by grassy leaves. The paperwhite is the most popular — and the easiest — bulb to force into early bloom indoors. All through the holidays you'll find pots of paperwhites blooming at the flower markets. In the South, and in Europe and North Africa, their native lands, the paperwhites bloom in gardens in late autumn and early winter.

The paperwhite belongs to the Tazetta class of narcissus, the historic Poetaz and Polyanthus daffodils. The sheer loveliness of the flower inspired the famous Greek legend about a youth named Narcissus, who had been given the gift of remaining beautiful his whole life. There was only one condition: he must never see his own reflection. Narcissus made the mistake of spurning the nymph Echo, and she took her revenge by having him coaxed to look at his image in a clear pool. Transfixed by his own beauty, he remained anchored before the image until he died. An exquisite flower bloomed where he had fallen, the narcissus.

At this time of the year, you'll find paperwhites as cut flowers. A bouquet of paperwhites and white roses tied with white satin ribbon makes an elegant birthday bouquet.

Or use potted paperwhites to make a beautiful birthday basket garden. Line a twelve-inch-deep round or square basket with

Birthdays December 16-23
Day & Year

_____

_____

_____

_____

_____

_____

heavy plastic and fill it
halfway with potting mix. Slip
the paperwhites into a corner
of the basket, being careful
not to disturb their roots.
Tuck in around them young
coleus plants,
wax bego-
nias, and
plant var-
iegated
ivy so that the
vines fall over the
sides.

105

Christmas Rose

This isn't the hellebore known as Christmas rose for its late winter blooming. Rather, it's the beautiful deep red rose that European tradition long ago joined to fresh holly, balsam, fir, and pine at this holiday season. Displays of red with evergreens brightened the dead of winter long before the Christian era. Romans decorated fir trees in honor of the return of light and life that begins after the winter solstice, December 21. An evergreen wreath is an ancient symbol of eternal life, a circle without beginning or end. Green leaves and berries that ripen to red in the dead of winter the Druids saw as proof that holly had magic powers, and the Christians adopted reds and greens into their mid winter celebration of birth and hope.

It's a Christian legend that associates red roses with the birth of the Christ. A little shepherdess tending sheep near Bethlehem heard about the birth of Jesus from the three Wise Men. She followed them to the manger and watched as they laid their gifts before the Infant. Love for the child filled her heart, but she had nothing to give and turned away, weeping. An angel appeared and touched the earth about the girl, and the ground was covered with lovely red roses. The infant turned from the gems and gold of the Wise Men and smiled as the girl heaped the red roses at his feet.

A freshly cut red rose is the flower of love and a beautiful gift for this week. All have some scent, but the most fragrant are 'Royalty' and 'Dakota'. 'Dakota' is known in Pennsylvania as 'Bucks County Beauties'. A red and white bicolor called 'Fire 'N Ice' is very pretty with holiday greens.

The birthday gift could be a single rose in a flower vial to hang on the tree, a wreath of evergreens studded with red roses in flower vials, or a florist's box filled with long-stemmed red roses.

Birthdays December 24-31
Day & Year

_____

_____

_____

_____

_____

Save the dried petals of gift bou-
quets to make a remembrance pot-
pourri: after the roses have peaked but
before they wilt, gather and dry the
petals and store them in an
airtight jar.

Acknowledgements and Bibliography

To our editor, Frances Tenenbaum, a lady full of wonder, and to designers Bob Barkin and Carlos Alexandre, our deepest thanks. Thanks as well to our manuscript editor, Luise Erdmann.

The authors are very grateful for assistance and information given by Joel Albizo, Society of American Florists; iris expert Libby Cross, Covington, Virginia; Tim Haley, Pike's Peak Greenhouses, Colorado Springs, Colorado; James Krone, Roses, Inc., Commercial Rose Growers' Association, Haslett, Minnesota; Holly Money-Collins, President, American Institute of Floral Designers, San Francisco; Marvel Sherrill, Director of Tours, Acres of Orchids, Rod McLellan Company, San Francisco; Rob Pennington, Conservatory Manager, US National Botanic Garden, Washington, D.C.

Behind this book are many hours of enchantment provided by other authors, notably Eleanor Sinclair Rohde, in *The Scented Garden;* Helen Van Pelt Wilson, in *The Fragrant Year;* Nelson Coon, in *Gardening for Fragrance;* Tovah Martin, in *The Essence of Paradise;* Elvin McDonald, in *The New Houseplant: Bringing the Garden Indoors;* Peter Loewer and Anne Moyer Halpin, in *Secrets of the Great Gardeners;* Cathy Wilkinson Barash, in *Evening Gardens;* Barron's and David Bateman, *The Garden, A Celebration.*

The authors have also drawn on Hériteau's *Potpourri and Other Fragrant Delights* (1973), edited by Helen Van Pelt Wilson.

The artist acknowledges the following works as reference for certain illustrations.

February	*Mezzetin* by Jean Antoine Watteau
March	*Annuciation* by Sandro Botticelli
April	*Napoleon Crossing the Alps* by J. L. David
June	*The Birth of Venus* by Botticelli
August	*The Love Letter* by Jean Honore Fragonard
September	*Woman's Head* by Erté
September	*Olive & Myrtle* by Henry Wood (photo)
December	*The Adoration of the Shepherds* by Louis Le Nain

Sources

If you can't find the flower you want locally, the catalogues offered by the suppliers listed here are reliable sources. You'll find other sources as well in Barbara J. Barton's *Gardening by Mail* (1994).

Brudy's Exotics
P.O. Box 820874
Houston, Texas 77282-0874

The Daffodil Mart
Route 3, Box 794
Gloucester, Virginia 23061

The Fragrant Path (fragrant flowers and shrubs)
P.O. Box 328
Fort Calhoun, Nebraska 68023

Logee's Greenhouses
141 North Street
Danielson, Connecticut 06239

Orchid Visitor Center
Rod McLellan Company
1450 El Camino Real
San Francisco, California 94080

Pikes Peak Greenhouses
P.O. Box 7070
Colorado Springs, Colorado 80933-7070

Thompson & Morgan Seed Co.
P.O. Box 1308
Jackson, New Jersey 08527

Tillotson's Roses
802 Brown's Valley Road
Watsonville, California 95076

Andre Viette Farm & Nursery
Route 1, Box 16
Fishersville, Virginia 22939

Wayside Gardens
1 Garden Lane
Hodges, South Carolina 29695-0001